Enclosure I

SEQUESTRATION: Observations on the Department of Defense's Approach in Fiscal Year 2013

GAO
U.S. GOVERNMENT ACCOUNTABILITY OFFICE

441 G St. N.W.
Washington, DC 20548

November 7, 2013

The Honorable Paul Ryan
Chairman
Committee on the Budget
House of Representatives

The Honorable Michael Turner
Chairman
The Honorable Loretta Sanchez
Ranking Member
Subcommittee on Tactical Air and Land Forces
Committee on Armed Services
House of Representatives

Sequestration: Observations on the Department of Defense's Approach in Fiscal Year 2013

The absence of legislation to reduce the federal budget deficit by at least $1.2 trillion triggered the sequestration process in section 251A of the Balanced Budget and Emergency Deficit Control Act of 1985 (BBEDCA), as amended. Pursuant to the BBEDCA, the President ordered sequestration of budgetary resources across non-exempt federal government accounts on March 1, 2013—five months into fiscal year 2013. In a March 2013 report to Congress, the Office of Management and Budget (OMB) calculated the overall reduction at $85.3 billion and estimated that the Department of Defense (DOD) would be required to take a 7.8 percent reduction in nonexempt defense discretionary funding, based on the continuing resolution in place at that time. Subsequent to the sequestration order, the Consolidated and Further Continuing Appropriations Act, 2013 provided DOD with a full appropriation for the remainder of fiscal year 2013.[1] As a result, OMB determined the total federal government sequestration reduction for fiscal year 2013 to be approximately $80 billion. This figure included reductions to DOD's resources of about $37 billion in discretionary appropriations and about $37.4 million in direct spending. DOD was required to apply the reductions to all programs, projects, and activities[2] within a budget account.[3] Table 1 below shows the allocation of spending reductions in DOD's non-exempt discretionary resources.

---

[1]Pub. L. No. 113-6 (2013).

[2]Certain defense-related programs, projects, and activities were exempted from sequestration in fiscal year 2013. For example, BBEDCA permits the President (subject to certain requirements) to exempt military personnel accounts, and OMB notified Congress of the President's intent to do so for fiscal year 2013 on July 31, 2012. Other defense-related accounts exempted from sequestration included the Department of Defense Medicare-Eligible Retiree Health Care Fund as well as all programs administered by the Department of Veterans Affairs.

[3]For DOD, the amount subject to sequestration included the fiscal year 2013 appropriation plus any unobligated balances in multi-year accounts from prior fiscal years that remain available for new obligations.

Table 1: Reductions in DOD Non-Exempt Discretionary Resources Due to Sequestration

Account (dollars in millions)	Sequestrable base[a]	Amount of reduction	Effective percent reduction[b]
Operation and maintenance	282,248	20,327	7.2%
Procurement	146,518	9,790	6.7%
Research, development, test and evaluation	74,565	6,055	8.1%
Military construction	18,611	821	4.4%
Other accounts[c]	5,766	224	3.9%
Total	527,708[d]	37,217	7.1%

Source: GAO analysis of DOD's June 2013 Sequestration Report.

[a]The sequestrable base is calculated by OMB. The amount shown reflects the fiscal year 2013 appropriation, which includes funding for overseas contingency operations, plus unobligated balances in multi-year accounts from prior fiscal years that remain available for new obligations.

[b]On March 1, 2013 OMB calculated the sequestrable base and reduction amounts based on the annualized amount set out in the continuing resolution then in effect. On March 26, 2013 the Consolidated and Further Continuing Appropriations Act, 2013 (Pub. L. No. 113-6) was enacted, providing different amounts of budget authority than were provided by the continuing resolution. According to DOD and OMB officials, the variation in percentage reductions across the discretionary accounts are the result of differences between the annualized continuing resolution amounts used in OMB's March 1st report and the enacted full-year appropriations.

[c]Other accounts include family housing, revolving and management funds, and certain trust funds.

[d]This figure does not include about $149.7 billion in discretionary resources for military personnel accounts, which were exempt from sequestration.

Subject to law and DOD financial management regulation, DOD has the authority to transfer funds between appropriation accounts and to reprogram funds within an appropriation account. DOD guidance requires that it seek approval from the congressional defense committees to reprogram funds above certain thresholds. This guidance also specifies circumstances where the department can reprogram funds without prior congressional approval if the cumulative increase or decrease of funds is within established thresholds.

You requested that we review DOD's approach and planning for managing the required spending reductions for fiscal year 2013. In this report, we describe the extent to which (1) DOD developed plans and methodologies to implement spending reductions in light of the Budget Control Act of 2011 and relevant guidance, including identifying potential impacts on U.S. military capabilities and DOD personnel and (2) DOD has made use of any reprogramming and transfer authorities to manage spending reductions during fiscal year 2013. In addition to reviewing DOD's overall approach to identify and manage the spending reductions, we focused on a number of specific areas within DOD, specifically civilian personnel; training and readiness; depot maintenance; base operating support; and procurement and research, development, test, and evaluation (RDT&E). Enclosure I provides the presentation detailing the observations of our review that we used in briefing your offices in September 2013.

To address our objectives, we reviewed guidance issued by the Office of the Secretary of Defense and the military services related to planning for and implementing sequestration. We also analyzed DOD program and financial data to identify spending reductions at the program, project, and activity level. We reviewed relevant documentation on DOD's analysis of alternatives for identifying specific spending reductions, including DOD guidance or criteria used to assess risks; potential impacts of sequestration on specific functions, programs, or other areas identified by DOD; and any mitigation strategies implemented or being considered by the department. To better understand DOD's approach, we conducted case study analyses in the areas of civilian personnel; depot maintenance; base operating support; training and readiness; and procurement and RDT&E, identifying specific planning steps and actions taken in each area as well as potential impacts from these decisions. Further, we analyzed financial management documents and other reports to determine the scope and basis of DOD's planned reprogramming and other transfers in fiscal year 2013.

We conducted this performance audit from March 2013 to November 2013 in accordance with generally accepted government auditing standards. Those standards require that we plan and perform the audit to obtain sufficient, appropriate evidence to provide a reasonable basis for our findings and conclusions based on our audit objectives. We believe that the evidence obtained provides a reasonable basis for our findings and conclusions based on our audit objectives.

Summary

Spending reductions under sequestration affected DOD's civilian workforce and many programs and functions, and required DOD to accept some risk in maintaining the readiness of military forces. However, DOD was able to mitigate some near-term effects of sequestration on its mission. Reduced spending levels required DOD to take actions such as furloughing most civilian employees for 6 days, cancelling or curtailing training for units that were not preparing to deploy by early in 2014, postponing some planned equipment maintenance at its depots and repairs or renovations of facilities, reducing some weapon system quantities or deferring modifications, and delaying system development and testing. DOD took various actions to plan for and implement sequestration, such as issuing guidance and establishing processes to identify priorities and evaluate alternatives for spending reductions. Generally, DOD's approach to sequestration was a short-term response focused on addressing the immediate funding reductions for fiscal year 2013. DOD was able to reduce spending levels for the remainder of fiscal year 2013 without making permanent changes, such as adjusting the size of its forces or canceling weapon systems programs. By setting priorities for funding and using available prior year unobligated balances to help meet required reductions, DOD was able to protect or minimize disruptions in certain key areas, such as maintaining support for ongoing operations and adhering to plans for major weapons systems acquisitions. In addition, because of the flexibility afforded from its reprogramming and transfer authorities, DOD was able to manage and, in some cases, later reverse some initial actions taken to implement the spending reductions, such as resuming aircraft training. DOD officials reported that some effects of the spending reductions were felt in fiscal year 2013 but that the full impact of sequestration would likely not be fully realized until fiscal year 2014 and beyond, and may vary by service. For example, DOD made adjustments to some of its procurement programs, such as deferring modifications or delaying system development and testing. DOD officials stated that some of these decisions may result in increased costs over the next few years.

DOD's Approach to Planning and Implementing Sequestration

Prior to and following the President's sequestration order, DOD took various actions to plan for and implement sequestration, such as issuing guidance and establishing processes to identify priorities and evaluate alternatives for spending reductions.

- In September 2012, DOD issued its first guidance, in part based on OMB guidance, which instructed its components to continue spending at normal levels. This guidance also instructed components not to take any steps to plan for sequestration. Officials from the military services told us that therefore they did not actively begin planning at that time. In January 2013, DOD instructed its components to begin implementing near-term actions, reversible if possible, to mitigate risks caused by the continuing resolution and potential sequestration while protecting programs such as wartime operations funding and Wounded Warrior programs focused on the health of servicemembers. Among other things, DOD's near-term actions included imposing hiring freezes and curtailing travel, training, and conferences.

- Following the President's March 1, 2013 sequestration order, DOD issued further guidance, such as technical instructions on allocating the spending reductions across programs, projects, and activities. It also took steps to set priorities and identify alternatives for applying spending reductions. To do so, DOD and the military services relied on existing governance structures and processes or established some new processes to obtain the input of senior officials to formulate proposed actions and reach decisions on spending reductions. For example, DOD relied on the Deputy Secretary of Defense's Defense Management Advisory Group, consisting of senior ranking officials, to evaluate proposals and coordinate implementation of sequestration across the department. In addition, the military services formed task forces or used other approaches to develop funding priorities and options for spending reductions. Through these mechanisms, DOD identified and began implementing various actions in the spring and early summer of 2013 to reduce spending levels for the remainder of the fiscal year, such as curtailing training for certain units, postponing some planned maintenance, reducing procurement quantities, and delaying system development and testing. DOD later made adjustments to its initial decisions, such as reinstating training.

In general, DOD's approach to sequestration was a short-term response to address the immediate spending reductions for fiscal year 2013. As such, the response was not a comprehensive review of potential long-term implications should sequestration occur in subsequent years. DOD officials noted that the department had begun some activities that may inform its decisions in fiscal year 2014 and beyond and may better position it to make more strategic choices should sequestration continue. For example, DOD recently completed the "Strategic Choices Management Review," which is intended to help inform DOD's preparation for alternative funding levels over a 10-year period. DOD has also begun development of the 2014 Quadrennial Defense Review, which will be a review of U.S. defense strategy, force structure, budget plans, and related policies.

As discussed above, we focused our review on selected areas. The following provides an overview of actions and potential impacts in each area we reviewed.

- *Civilian Personnel* – On May 14, 2013, the Secretary of Defense directed that "most" DOD federal civilians be furloughed for up to 11 days beginning the week of July 8, 2013, except that exemptions be granted across the department for specific personnel, including, shipyard personnel, National Intelligence Program personnel, and employees necessary to protect life and property. On August 6, 2013, the Secretary of Defense directed that the number of furlough days be reduced to 6. According to DOD, this reduction was possible because additional funding became available through transfers and reprogrammings and other DOD management actions. As of September 2013, DOD estimated that 640,592 civilians would be furloughed for 6 days, for an estimated total cost reduction of approximately $1.2 billion. Senior DOD officials have noted that furloughs have the potential to negatively affect productivity, morale, and local economies.

- *Training and Readiness* – DOD guidance directed the components to implement actions to mitigate risks and minimize the harmful effects of sequestration on operations and unit readiness. In response, the military services prioritized training programs for deployed and next-to-deploy forces and took actions to cancel or limit training for forces not preparing to deploy in early 2014. For example, the Army curtailed training for all units except those deployed, preparing to deploy, or stationed overseas, and the Navy limited flight training for non-deploying units. In some cases, the services reversed actions that were originally taken to implement fiscal year 2013 spending reductions. For example, in April 2013, the Air Force initially ceased flight operations for about one-third of its active duty combat units. In July 2013, the Air Force resumed flight operations for these units based on approved plans to reprogram funds. As a result of their planned actions, the services identified potential impacts on readiness, including an increase in the number of non-deployable units, decreased surge capacity, and delays in their ability to reconstitute core mission readiness. DOD and service officials stated that they expect to see more significant impacts in fiscal year 2014 and beyond as the effects of the spending reductions from sequestration in fiscal year 2013 become more apparent.

- *Depot Maintenance* – DOD prioritized funding to maintain equipment readiness for ongoing operations. However, reduced funding levels due to sequestration required some of the services to defer depot maintenance that had been planned for fiscal year 2013 until future years. For example, Air Force officials estimated that about $100 million in maintenance for the active duty force was deferred from their public depots. Further, the Army released depot personnel and the public depots were also subject to department-wide hiring freezes. If these actions continue into future years, service officials anticipate potential impacts such as equipment readiness shortfalls and delays resetting the force, increases in depot rates—leading to more expensive maintenance costs—and reduced depot workforce capabilities.

- *Base Operating Support* – Service installation commands and other organizations responsible for oversight of base operating support issued guidance that outlined areas where spending reductions could be implemented—such as deferring building sustainment, delaying the renewal of contracts, and reducing electricity usage—without sacrificing the protection of life, health, and safety. Individual installation commanders retained substantial flexibility in how to implement cuts, including which base support services to reduce or eliminate. Our review found that many reductions focused on facilities' sustainment, restoration, and modernization accounts. For example, the Air Force took a variety of actions—including canceling mold remediation and other environmental projects, deferring repairs to alarm systems, and reducing recreation and fitness programs. Service officials expressed concerns about the adverse effects of these actions, such as the potential for high future costs to remedy degradation of DOD facilities.

- *Procurement and RDT&E* – Of DOD's nearly $16 billion reduction to its procurement and RDT&E accounts, about $10 billion came from procurement funds and about $6 billion came from RDT&E funds. DOD used approximately $5 billion in prior year unobligated balances to help cover the sequestration reductions. For the remaining reductions, DOD officials stated that they typically made short-term adjustments to programs, such as changes to system quantities, deferred modifications, or delayed system development and testing, rather than making more severe changes, such as canceling programs. For example, both the Apache (block III) and Kiowa Warrior Army helicopter programs reported that they had to cut one aircraft from their fiscal year 2013 buy. DOD officials stated that some of these decisions may result in increased costs over the next few years.

DOD's Use of Transfer and Reprogramming Authorities

Since the President's sequestration order, DOD has made use of available reprogramming and transfer authorities in large part to meet overseas contingency operations-related funding needs. The Consolidated and Further Continuing Appropriations Act, 2013[4] provided DOD with $7.5 billion in broad authority to transfer funds between appropriations in fiscal year 2013. Of this amount, $3.5 billion was special transfer authority for purposes related to overseas contingency operations and $4 billion was general transfer authority. These amounts were generally consistent with the amounts of broad transfer authority that Congress provided to DOD in fiscal years 2011 and 2012. DOD submitted two requests to Congress totaling $9.4 billion dated May 17, 2013, to transfer and reprogram funds that had been appropriated for fiscal year 2013.[5] On July 19, 2013, DOD submitted two additional requests to Congress totaling about $1.5 billion. These requests identified replacement sources for the transfer or reprogramming requests originally submitted on May 17, 2013 but disapproved at that time by the congressional defense committees, as well as new requests to transfer and reprogram fiscal year 2013 funds. As of September 2013, DOD told us that the relevant congressional committees had approved about $8.6 billion of DOD's total transfer and reprogramming requests.

Officials told us that although the department did not use its reprogramming and transfer authority to directly mitigate the effects of sequestration, the flexibility to transfer or reprogram funds to cover expenses for overseas contingency operations that otherwise would have been funded by other areas in the budget allowed DOD to reverse some actions taken to achieve spending reductions.[6] For example, as noted above, Air Force officials stated that, based on approvals to reprogram funds, the service was able to resume flight operations for some active duty combat units.

---

[4]Pub. L. No. 113-6 (2013).

[5]These requests proposed to transfer about $7.3 billion between accounts using DOD's broad transfer authorities and, according to DOD officials, the remaining $2.1 billion represented large reprogrammings within budget accounts and transfers from DOD's foreign currency fluctuations account.

[6]DOD officials told us that changing assumptions for overseas contingency operations, such as the increased costs associated with drawdown-related contract services in Afghanistan, have led to higher than projected costs for fiscal year 2013.

Agency Comments and Our Evaluation

We provided DOD with a draft of this report for comment. DOD concurred with our report. DOD also provided technical comments that we incorporated where appropriate.

- - - - -

We are sending copies of this report to the appropriate congressional committees and to the Secretary of Defense. The report is also available at no charge on the GAO website at http://www.gao.gov.

If you or your staff have any questions concerning this report, please contact Sharon Pickup at (202) 512-9619 or pickups@gao.gov or Michael Sullivan at (202) 512-4841 or sullivanm@gao.gov. Contact points for our offices of Congressional Relations and Public Affairs may be found on the last page of this report. GAO staff who made key contributors to this report are listed in enclosure II.

Sharon L. Pickup
Director
Defense Capabilities and Management

Michael J. Sullivan
Director
Acquisition and Sourcing Management

Enclosures – 2

SEQUESTRATION: Observations on the Department of Defense's Approach in Fiscal Year 2013

Overview

- Introduction

- Observations

  - Objective 1: DOD Planning to Implement Sequestration

    - Civilian Personnel Case Study

    - Training and Readiness Case Study

    - Depot Maintenance Case Study

    - Base Operating Support Case Study

    - Research, Development, Test and Evaluation (RDT&E) and Procurement Case Study

  - Objective 2: Use of Reprogramming and Transfer Authorities to Address Sequestration

  - Appendix I: Background on Statutes Related to Sequestration

Introduction to the Engagement

GAO conducted this work in response to requests from the

- House Budget Committee

- House Armed Services Subcommittee on Tactical Air and Land Forces

To address these requests, we evaluated the extent to which

1. DOD has developed plans and methodologies to implement spending reductions in light of the Budget Control Act of 2011 and relevant guidance, including identifying any impacts on U.S. military capabilities and DOD personnel.

2. DOD has made use of any reprogramming or other transfer authorities to manage any spending reductions during fiscal year 2013.

Introduction to Sequestration

- "Sequestration" is a process of presidentially directed, largely across-the-board spending reductions under which budget authority is reduced to enforce certain budget policy goals.

- Various statutes are relevant to the current implementation of sequestration. They are summarized in Appendix I. These statutes include

  - **Balanced Budget and Emergency Deficit Control Act of 1985** (BBEDCA), Pub. L. No. 99-177 (1985)

  - **Budget Control Act of 2011** (BCA), Pub. L. No. 112-25 (2011)

  - **Sequestration Transparency Act of 2012**, Pub. L. No. 112-155 (2012)

  - **American Taxpayer Relief Act of 2012**, Pub. L. No. 112-240 (2013)

- Certain defense-related programs, projects, and activities (PPAs) were exempt from sequestration, such as military personnel accounts,[1] DOD's Medicare-Eligible Retiree Health Care Fund, and all programs administered by the Department of Veterans Affairs.

---

[1]BBEDCA permits the President (subject to certain requirements) to exempt military personnel accounts, and OMB notified Congress of the President's intent to do so for fiscal year 2013 on July 31, 2012.

Introduction to Sequestration (cont.)

- DOD developed definitions for PPAs—across which spending reductions must be evenly applied.

    - For operation and maintenance (O&M) accounts, PPA is defined at the appropriation account level (e.g., O&M, Navy; O&M, Army).

    - For all other accounts, PPA is defined as the most specific level of budget item identified in the Consolidated and Further Continuing Appropriations Act, 2013, classified annexes and explanatory statements to that act, or certain agency budget justification materials. That level of detail would include individual acquisition programs and military construction projects.

- In a report dated March 1, 2013, OMB calculated the sequestrable base and reduction amounts based on the annualized amount set out in the continuing resolution then in effect.[2] OMB calculated DOD's reduction as 7.8 percent for nonexempt defense discretionary funding and 7.9 percent for nonexempt defense direct spending.

- On March 26, 2013, the **Consolidated and Further Continuing Appropriations Act, 2013** (Pub. L. No. 113-6) provided DOD with a full appropriation for the remainder of fiscal year 2013. As a result, on May 15, 2013, OMB determined that DOD's fiscal year 2013 total sequestration would be adjusted from $41 billion to $37 billion.[3]

- Under sequestration, properly designated funding for overseas contingency operations is subject to reductions, but such funding raises the BCA discretionary spending caps.[4]

---

[2] OMB, *OMB Report to the Congress on the Joint Committee Sequestration for FY 2013* (March 1, 2013).

[3] OMB and DOD officials indicated that the $4 billion reduction in DOD's sequestration amount resulted primarily from the application of section 253(f)(2) of BBEDCA (codified as amended at 2 U.S.C. § 903(f)(2)). Section 253(f)(2) of BBEDCA provides for a reduction in the amount of sequestration for certain accounts initially funded under a part-year continuing resolution when the enacted full-year appropriation is less than the baseline for that account. OMB defined the baseline in this context as the annualized part-year continuing resolution amount minus the sequestration amount calculated in OMB's March 1st Report.

[4] If both Congress (by law) and the President designate funding as overseas contingency operations funding, it is considered overseas contingency operations funding for the purposes of adjustments to sequestration caps.

GAO-14-177R Sequestration

Introduction to Sequestration (cont.)

- Total federal government sequestration for fiscal year 2013 amounts to approximately $80 billion.
- Reductions in DOD's nonexempt discretionary funding amount to $37 billion, reducing new budget authority for DOD in fiscal year 2013 by $31 billion.[5] The remaining $6 billion is composed of currently available prior year unobligated balances. Based on OMB's calculations, the reductions are applied to DOD accounts as follows:

Table 1: Reductions in DOD Non-Exempt Discretionary Resources Due to Sequestration

Account ($ in millions)	Sequestrable Base[6]	Amount of Reduction	Effective % Reduction[7]
Operation and Maintenance	282,248	20,327	7.2%
Procurement	146,518	9,790	6.7%
Research, Development, Test and Evaluation	74,565	6,055	8.1%
Military Construction	18,611	821	4.4%
Other Accounts[8]	5,766	224	3.9%
Total	527,708[9]	37,217	7.1%

Source: GAO analysis of DOD's June 2013 Sequestration Report.

---

[5]In addition, DOD's reductions included about $37 million in direct spending. Direct spending affected includes a trust fund for commissary surcharge collections.
[6]The sequestrable base is calculated by OMB. The amount shown reflects the fiscal year 2013 appropriation, which includes funding for overseas contingency operations, plus unobligated balances in multi-year accounts from prior fiscal years that remain available for new obligations.
[7]On March1, 2013 OMB calculated the sequestrable base and reduction amounts based on the annualized amount set out in the continuing resolution then in effect. On March 26, 2013 the Consolidated and Further Continuing Appropriations Act, 2013 (Pub. L. No. 113-6) was enacted, providing different amounts of budget authority than were provided by the continuing resolution. According to DOD and OMB officials, the varying percentage reductions across the discretionary accounts are the result of differences between the annualized continuing resolution amounts used in OMB's March 1st report and the enacted full-year appropriations.
[8]Other accounts include family housing, revolving and management funds, and certain trust funds.
[9]This figure does not include about $149.7 billion in discretionary resources for DOD's military personnel accounts, which were exempt from sequestration.

Observations: Objective 1
DOD Planning to Implement Sequestration

DOD provided general guidance related to sequestration to the military services and other components, beginning in September 2012. For example,

- According to DOD officials, DOD issued its first guidance in September 2012, in part based on OMB's July 2012 guidance that instructed agencies to continue normal spending and operations. DOD's September 2012, guidance instructed components to continue spending at normal levels and not to take any steps to plan for implementation of sequestration.[10] Officials from the military services told us that, accordingly, they did not reduce spending or actively begin planning for sequestration until December 2012.

- On January 10, 2013, DOD instructed components to

  - implement near-term actions, such as freezing civilian hiring; reducing base operating spending; and curtailing spending on travel, training, and conferences.

  - protect certain programs, such as wartime operations, wounded warrior programs, family programs, and select programs associated with the current defense strategy.

The following two slides show the sequence of guidance OMB issued before and after the President's sequestration order and the corresponding DOD guidance.

---

[10]Spending levels were based on the continuing resolution in effect at that time.

Observations: Objective 1

DOD Planning to Implement Sequestration (cont.)

Figure 1: DOD and OMB Guidance Prior to Sequestration Order

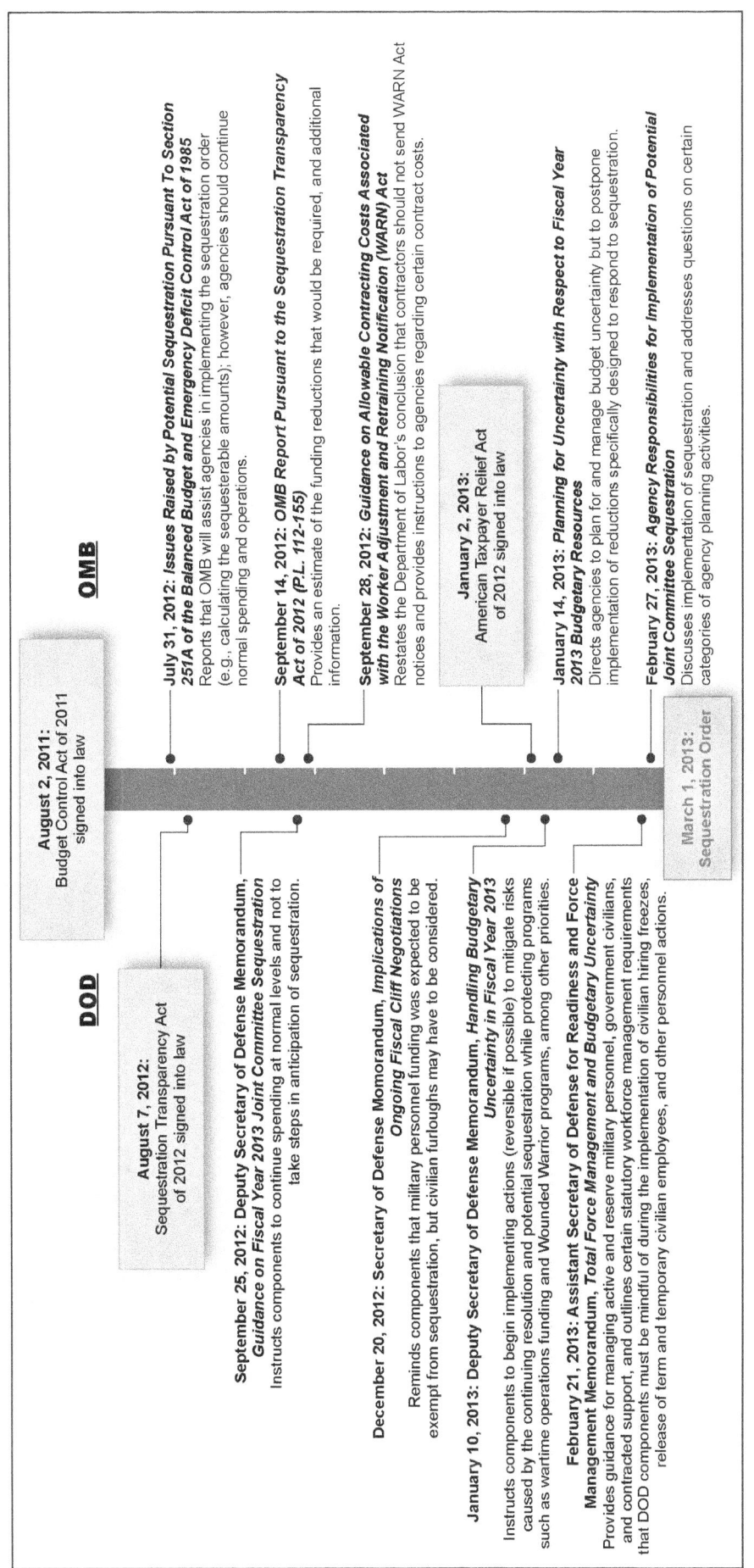

Source: GAO analysis of DOD and OMB information.

DOD Planning to Implement Sequestration Order

Figure 2: DOD and OMB Guidance Following Sequestration Order

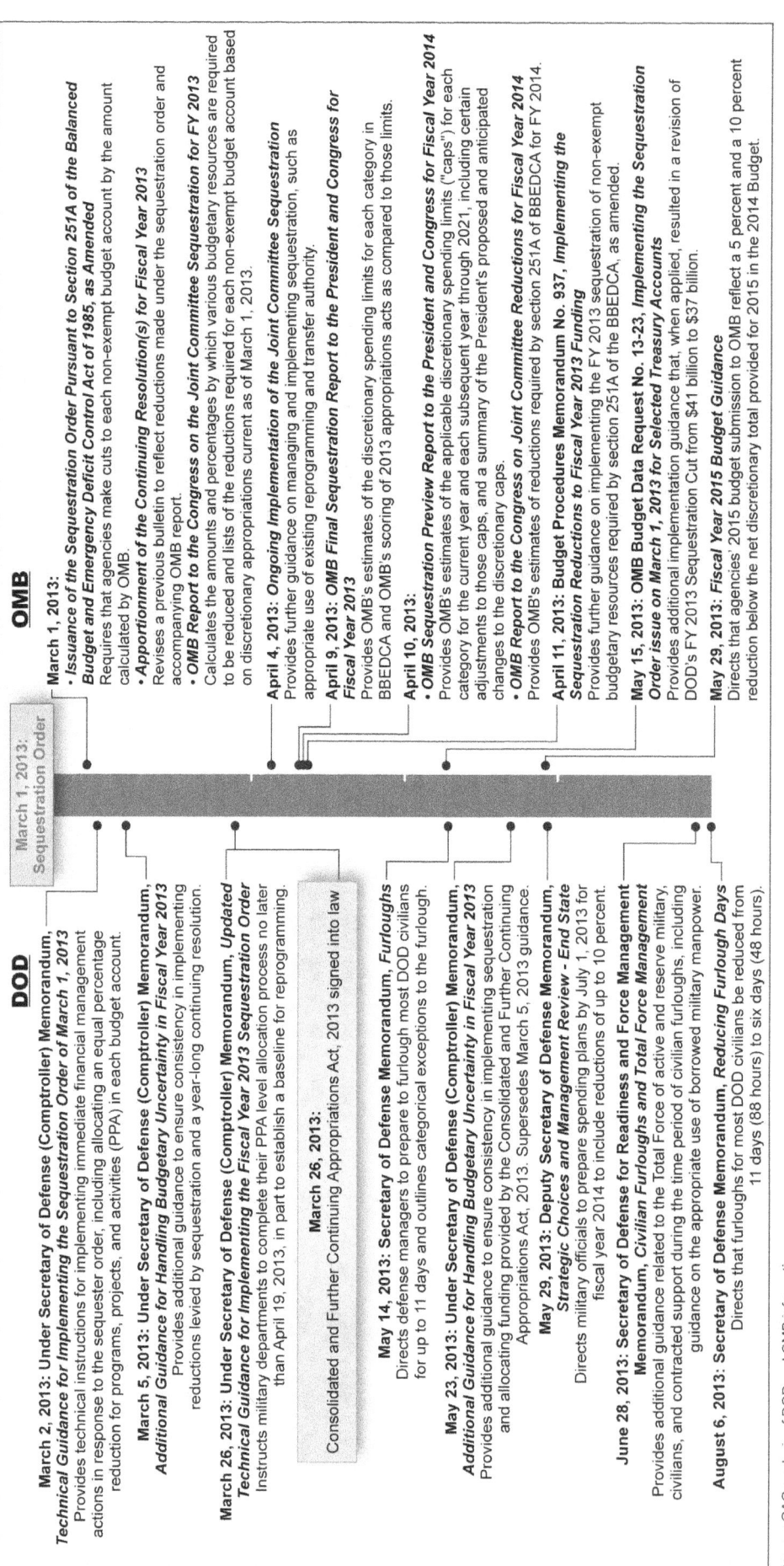

DOD

March 2, 2013: Under Secretary of Defense (Comptroller) Memorandum, *Technical Guidance for Implementing the Sequestration Order of March 1, 2013*
Provides technical instructions for implementing immediate financial management actions in response to the sequester order, including allocating an equal percentage reduction for programs, projects, and activities (PPA) in each budget account.

March 5, 2013: Under Secretary of Defense (Comptroller) Memorandum, *Additional Guidance for Handling Budgetary Uncertainty in Fiscal Year 2013*
Provides additional guidance to ensure consistency in implementing reductions levied by sequestration and a year-long continuing resolution.

March 26, 2013: Under Secretary of Defense (Comptroller) Memorandum, *Updated Technical Guidance for Implementing the Fiscal Year 2013 Sequestration Order*
Instructs military departments to complete their PPA level allocation process no later than April 19, 2013, in part to establish a baseline for reprogramming.

March 26, 2013: Consolidated and Further Continuing Appropriations Act, 2013 signed into law

May 14, 2013: Secretary of Defense Memorandum, *Furloughs*
Directs defense managers to prepare to furlough most DOD civilians for up to 11 days and outlines categorical exceptions to the furlough.

May 23, 2013: Under Secretary of Defense (Comptroller) Memorandum, *Additional Guidance for Handling Budgetary Uncertainty in Fiscal Year 2013*
Provides additional guidance to ensure consistency in implementing sequestration and allocating additional funding provided by the Consolidated and Further Continuing Appropriations Act, 2013. Supersedes March 5, 2013 guidance.

May 29, 2013: Deputy Secretary of Defense Memorandum, *Strategic Choices and Management Review - End State*
Directs military officials to prepare spending plans by July 1, 2013 for fiscal year 2014 to include reductions of up to 10 percent.

June 28, 2013: Secretary of Defense for Readiness and Force Management Memorandum, *Civilian Furloughs and Total Force Management*
Provides additional guidance related to the Total Force of active and reserve military, civilians, and contracted support during the time period of civilian furloughs, including guidance on the appropriate use of borrowed military manpower.

August 6, 2013: Secretary of Defense Memorandum, *Reducing Furlough Days*
Directs that furloughs for most DOD civilians be reduced from 11 days (88 hours) to six days (48 hours).

March 1, 2013: Sequestration Order

OMB

March 1, 2013:
• *Issuance of the Sequestration Order Pursuant to Section 251A of the Balanced Budget and Emergency Deficit Control Act of 1985, as Amended*
Requires that agencies make cuts to each non-exempt budget account by the amount calculated by OMB.
• *Apportionment of the Continuing Resolution(s) for Fiscal Year 2013*
Revises a previous bulletin to reflect reductions made under the sequestration order and accompanying OMB report.
• *OMB Report to the Congress on the Joint Committee Sequestration for FY 2013*
Calculates the amounts and percentages by which various budgetary resources are required to be reduced and lists of the reductions required for each non-exempt budget account based on discretionary appropriations current as of March 1, 2013.

April 4, 2013: *Ongoing Implementation of the Joint Committee Sequestration*
Provides further guidance on managing and implementing sequestration, such as appropriate use of existing reprogramming and transfer authority.

April 9, 2013: *OMB Final Sequestration Report to the President and Congress for Fiscal Year 2013*
Provides OMB's estimates of the discretionary spending limits for each category in BBEDCA and OMB's scoring of 2013 appropriations acts as compared to those limits.

April 10, 2013:
• *OMB Sequestration Preview Report to the President and Congress for Fiscal Year 2014*
Provides OMB's estimates of the applicable discretionary spending limits ("caps") for each category for the current year and each subsequent year through 2021, including certain adjustments to those caps, and a summary of the President's proposed and anticipated changes to the discretionary caps.
• *OMB Report to the Congress on Joint Committee Reductions for Fiscal Year 2014*
Provides OMB's estimates of reductions required by section 251A of BBEDCA for FY 2014.

April 11, 2013: Budget Procedures Memorandum No. 937, *Implementing the Sequestration Reductions to Fiscal Year 2013 Funding*
Provides further guidance on implementing the FY 2013 sequestration of non-exempt budgetary resources required by section 251A of the BBEDCA, as amended.

May 15, 2013: OMB Budget Data Request No. 13-23, *Implementing the Sequestration Order issue on March 1, 2013 for Selected Treasury Accounts*
Provides additional implementation guidance that, when applied, resulted in a revision of DOD's FY 2013 Sequestration Cut from $41 billion to $37 billion.

May 29, 2013: *Fiscal Year 2015 Budget Guidance*
Directs that agencies' 2015 budget submission to OMB reflect a 5 percent and a 10 percent reduction below the net discretionary total provided for 2015 in the 2014 Budget.

Source: GAO analysis of DOD and OMB information.

Observations: Objective 1
DOD Planning to Implement Sequestration (cont.)

In general, DOD has established processes to identify priorities and evaluate alternatives for implementing fiscal year 2013 sequestration spending reductions.

- At the senior level, DOD is utilizing the Deputy Secretary of Defense's Deputy's Management Action Group to coordinate the approach to sequestration across DOD.

- The military services established processes beginning in December 2012 to identify priorities and evaluate alternatives.

  - The Army utilized a process, referred to as a sequestration "Rehearsal of Concept" drill to develop a list of funding priorities.

  - The Air Force established a "Sequestration Task Force" to develop a plan for implementing sequestration reductions.

  - The Navy established a two-tiered approach to planning for a range of funding scenarios to identify potential ways to cut costs while preserving the current deployment schedule for fiscal year 2013.

  - The Marine Corps used existing processes to review and approve options based on various spending reductions.

- The services have utilized these and other processes to monitor the execution of funds and revise priorities, as appropriate.

Observations: Objective 1

DOD Planning to Implement Sequestration (cont.)

- DOD's approach to sequestration was a short-term response focused on addressing the immediate funding reductions for fiscal year 2013. In general, this response was not a comprehensive review of potential long-term implications should sequestration occur in subsequent years.

- DOD officials noted that the President's exemption of military personnel accounts from sequestration—as allowed by legislation—and DOD's decisions to protect certain programs, such as overseas contingency operations, had the effect of reducing the number of areas where spending reductions could be applied.

- DOD took various actions to reduce spending levels for the remainder of the fiscal year, such as curtailing or postponing certain activities. DOD did not make permanent changes like adjusting force structure or cancelling weapon system programs. For example:

  - DOD curtailed training for certain units and postponed some planned maintenance. These actions required DOD to accept risk to readiness in fiscal year 2013 and have pushed some costs into future years.

  - DOD used significant portions of available unobligated balances from prior years for its procurement and RDT&E accounts.

  - DOD later made adjustments to its initial decisions, such as reinstating training.

- As a result of these actions, DOD may have to consider alternative actions to make spending reductions in fiscal year 2014 should sequestration continue.

Observations: Objective 1

DOD Planning to Implement Sequestration (cont.)

- DOD's fiscal year 2014 budget request (about $606 billion) did not take into account the additional reductions required by section 251A of BBEDCA.

  - On May 29, 2013, the Deputy Secretary of Defense issued guidance directing the military services and other components to develop additional options that are 10 percent below the President's fiscal year 2014 budget request. On the same date, OMB issued guidance directing agencies to develop similar options when planning for the fiscal year 2015 budget.

  - The Senate Armed Services Committee directed DOD to provide information, by July 1, 2013, on how it would apply sequestration to its fiscal year 2014 budget request (about $52 billion in reductions). On July 10, 2013, the Secretary of Defense responded to this request and sent a letter to the committee identifying various types of actions DOD would consider should sequestration occur in fiscal year 2014.

- DOD has begun some activities that may inform its decisions for fiscal year 2014 and beyond and may better position it to make more strategic choices, should sequestration continue.

  - DOD completed the "Strategic Choices Management Review" in June 2013, which was intended to help inform DOD's preparation for alternative funding levels over a 10-year period.

  - DOD has begun conducting the 2014 Quadrennial Defense Review, which will review U.S. defense strategy, force structure, budget plans, and related policies.

  - According to DOD officials, the department's approach to implementing sequestration in fiscal year 2014 would likely include short-term options—as occurred for fiscal year 2013—but may also include options for longer-term, more permanent changes, such as adjustments to force structure.

Observations: Objective 1
DOD Planning to Implement Sequestration (cont.)

It is difficult to attribute specific impacts directly to fiscal year 2013 sequestration reductions, because other actions have also affected DOD funding levels and programs. For example:

- In May 2010, the Secretary of Defense directed DOD to undertake a department-wide initiative to assess how the department is staffed, organized, and operated, with the goal of reducing excess overhead costs and reinvesting any resulting savings. DOD is still in the process of implementing the specific actions resulting from this initiative.

- For the first 6 months of fiscal year 2013, DOD operated under a continuing resolution, which limited its budget authority and flexibility to move funds.

- DOD officials told us that changing assumptions for overseas contingency operations, such as the increased costs associated with drawdown-related contract services in Afghanistan, have led to higher than projected costs for fiscal year 2013.

DOD officials stated that there is an interrelationship among the types of spending reductions that must be considered when determining how to implement these reductions. For example, service officials told us that

- Reduced depot maintenance funds and civilian furloughs affect the services' ability to effectively execute training; funding could be available for flying hours, but these flying hours might not be executed because airframes could be grounded for maintenance or training ranges closed due to furloughs of civilian personnel, such as instructors or simulator operators. Many installation support services, such as legal support and financial management, will be affected by civilian furloughs.

The next 16 slides present information on background, planning processes, actions taken, and potential impacts of sequestration for five case study areas that we reviewed as part of our work.

The following four case study areas are associated with DOD's operation and maintenance accounts:

- **Civilian Personnel** - DOD's civilian workforce has a wide variety of responsibilities and duties including, among other things, developing policy, gathering intelligence, managing finances, maintaining weapon systems and awarding contracts, and overseeing contractor performance. Civilian personnel are largely funded through operation and maintenance funds, but some personnel are funded through other appropriations, such as RDT&E.

- **Training and Readiness** - To maintain a trained and ready force, DOD relies heavily on operation and maintenance funds, which fund deployments, training, and maintenance, among other activities.

- **Depot Maintenance** - Depot maintenance is the highest level of maintenance within DOD and generally refers to major maintenance and repair actions on weapon systems and equipment.

- **Base Operating Support** - Installation support services vary across the military services, but each military service provides support to U.S. military bases for many different kinds of functions, including maintenance of base facilities and equipment, security, child care, and youth programs.

The fifth case study area is associated with some of DOD's investment accounts:

- **RDT&E and Procurement** – RDT&E funds finance research, development, and test and evaluation efforts performed by contractors and government installations to develop equipment and weapon systems. Procurement funds are used to purchase ships, aircraft, ground vehicles, etc., after these are developed.

Observations

Case Study 1: Civilian Personnel

Planning Process

Officials stated that the decision to furlough many, but not all civilian employees was made by the Secretary of Defense with input from various sources, including the military departments, Office of the Comptroller, and Office of the Under Secretary of Defense for Personnel and Readiness.

Actions Taken

- On May 14, 2013, the Secretary of Defense directed that "most" DOD federal civilians be furloughed for up to 11 days (1 day per week for the remainder of the fiscal year) beginning the week of July 8, 2013.

- The Secretary of Defense also directed that categorical exceptions be granted across the department and granted specific exceptions to each of the military departments and elsewhere within the department. For example, employees necessary to protect life and property, shipyard personnel, and National Intelligence Program personnel were exempted from DOD furloughs.

- In the implementation of civilian furloughs, commanders and managers were given the authority to develop the specifics of furlough procedures in order to minimize adverse mission effects and also limit the harm to morale and productivity.

Observations

Case Study 1: Civilian Personnel (cont.)

Potential Impacts

- On August 6, 2013, the Secretary of Defense directed that the number of furlough days be reduced to 6. According to DOD, this reduction was possible due to additional funding that became available through transfers and reprogrammings and other DOD management actions.

- As of September 2013, DOD estimated that 640,592 of approximately 770,000 civilians were furloughed for 6 days at an estimated total cost reduction of approximately $1.2 billion (estimated average of $300/per furlough day). With civilian personnel facing one furlough day per week starting July 8, 2013, staff realized a 20 percent pay reduction each week while furloughed.

- Senior DOD officials have noted that furloughs have the potential to negatively affect productivity, morale, and local economies.

- GAO recently initiated an engagement, in response to a mandate,[11] to assess DOD's implementation of furloughs.

---

[11]H. Rep. No.113-102 to accompany H.R. 1960, a bill for the National Defense Authorization Act of Fiscal Year 2014 (Jun. 7, 2013).

Observations

Case Study 2: Training and Readiness

Planning Process

In planning for sequestration and related budget uncertainties, DOD directed its components to implement actions to mitigate risks and to structure those actions to minimize harmful effects on operations and unit readiness.

- In response, the services prioritized certain areas for funding and identified lower priority activities for funding reductions.

- The services' priorities were to support training requirements for deployed and next-to-deploy forces, as well as other defense priorities.

Actions Taken

The types of adjustments the services made varied in detail but often fell along similar lines, including

- canceling or limiting training for forces not preparing to deploy in fiscal year 2014

- shortening, canceling, or modifying scheduled deployments.

Observations

Case Study 2: Training and Readiness (cont.)

- *Examples of Specific Training Actions*

  According to DOD and military service reports and analyses, and based on our discussions with departmental officials, some examples of actions that the services have taken include:

  - **Army**

    Curtailing training for all units except those deployed, preparing to deploy, or stationed overseas, and canceling training at combat training centers for all but those units that are preparing to deploy for ongoing operations.

  - **Air Force**

    Initially ceasing flight operations for about one-third of active duty combat Air Force units in April 2013. Based on the decision to reprogram funds, these units re-started flight operations in July 2013, according to Air Force officials.

  - **Navy**

    Limiting flight training for non-deploying units.

  - **Marine Corps**

    Reducing the number of forces participating in overseas training exercises.

Observations

Case Study 2: Training and Readiness (cont.)

Potential Impacts

- The services identified potential impacts from sequestration, including
  - increased number of non-deployable units
  - decreased surge capacity, i.e., ability to quickly meet additional requirements with ready forces
  - decreased availability of critical capabilities where skills and qualifications atrophy quickly
  - delays in their ability to reconstitute core mission readiness after a decade of ongoing operations

- DOD and the services expect to see some specific impacts of fiscal year 2013 reductions in the reported readiness levels of their forces in the next couple of months. However, DOD and the services expect to see more significant impacts in fiscal year 2014 and beyond as the effects of sequestration become more apparent.

- DOD and the services have begun conducting some assessments of readiness impacts likely to result from sequestration. For example, Office of the Secretary of Defense officials stated that they have begun to review what the effects of sequestration are likely to be on DOD's ability to provide forces to meet combatant command requirements, but these efforts are in early stages.

- In response to mandates from the House and Senate Armed Services Committees, GAO will be reviewing trends in military readiness, including the impact of sequestration.[12]

---

[12]See H.R. Rep. No.113-102 at 124-125 (Jun. 7, 2013), and S. Rep. No. 113-44 at 89-90 (Jun. 20, 2013)

Background

DOD operates 17 major public depots that perform maintenance and associated activities on weapon systems and equipment.[13] While private contractors also perform depot maintenance, our analysis focused on maintenance at DOD's public depots. DOD's depot maintenance is subject to statutory requirements that include (1) the "50-50" provision limiting the amount of funding for maintenance performed by non-federal government (private) personnel and facilities (10 U.S.C. § 2466) and (2) a requirement that sufficient workload be performed in public depots to maintain a core capability (10 U.S.C. § 2464).

Planning Process and Actions Taken

According to officials, sequestration planning for depot maintenance occurred as part of the overall processes established by each service. Readiness for ongoing operations was generally considered a key priority in making maintenance funding decisions.

Deferred Maintenance

- Due to reduced funding, some of the services deferred depot maintenance that was planned for fiscal year 2013 until future years. For example, as of September 2013, Air Force officials estimated that about $100 million related to maintenance projects for its active duty force was deferred from their public depots, including 9 aircraft and 16 engines. Also, at that time, Army officials estimated that about $152 million of maintenance was deferred from their depots, including tracked and wheeled combat vehicles, communications and electronics equipment, and other weapons.[14]

---

[13]Depot maintenance is, subject to certain exceptions, material maintenance or repair requiring the overhaul, upgrading, or rebuilding of parts, assemblies, or subassemblies, and the testing and reclamation of equipment as necessary, regardless of the source of funds for the maintenance or repair or the location at which the maintenance or repair is performed.
[14]Army officials estimated that approximately another $58 million of depot maintenance was deferred from fiscal year 2013, but they did not know how much of this maintenance would have been performed at their public depots.

Case Study 3: Depot Maintenance (cont.)

- In response to Senate direction, the Office of the Secretary of Defense is preparing a report on DOD's deferred depot maintenance.[15] According to a DOD official, the report will include an estimate of total deferred maintenance at the end of fiscal year 2013, including any remaining deferred work from prior years that was not completed during the fiscal year.

Furloughs, Personnel Reductions, and Hiring Freezes

- As with most of DOD's civilian personnel, depot employees were furloughed for 6 days in fiscal year 2013, with the exception of civilians at the Navy's four shipyards.

- The Army depots reduced permanent civilian, temporary, term, and/or contract employees. Army officials stated that the depots reduced their workforce levels by about 3,250 personnel in fiscal year 2013.[16] According to officials, sequestration accelerated these personnel reductions.[17]

- The services implemented service-wide civilian hiring freezes, with limited hiring exceptions available for mission-critical activities.[18] Therefore, the depots could not hire and train personnel for future needs, and some positions remained vacant. As an example, Navy officials estimated that, as of the end of fiscal year 2013, the aviation depot workforce was understaffed by about 600 personnel.

---

[15]See S.Rep.112-173 to accompany S. 3254 a bill for the National Defense Authorization Act for Fiscal Year 2013 (Jun. 4, 2012).
[16]About 1,200 were permanent civilian personnel who either accepted a Voluntary Early Retirement Authority/Voluntary Separation Incentive Payment offer or left through normal attrition.
[17]Officials had already projected changes in the future amount of work at the Army depots due to the drawdown of combat operations.
[18]The hiring freeze for the Navy shipyards was lifted in June 2013.

Case Study 3: Depot Maintenance (cont.)

Potential Impacts

- Service officials anticipated some depot maintenance impacts as a result of fiscal year 2013 sequestration. These impacts are likely to vary by service, depot, and individual weapon system, depending on factors such as the final allocation of fiscal year 2013 operations and maintenance funding based on spending reductions, decisions regarding the use of these funds for depot maintenance, and the extent of depot personnel actions.

  - For example, the civilian furlough period caused delays in maintaining equipment. According to Navy aviation depot officials, delivery dates were delayed throughout the furlough period and about 36 aircraft and 87 engines and engine components were not delivered in fiscal year 2013 as planned. While these delays affected various equipment, aircraft already constrained by low readiness rates—such as the F/A-18—experienced the greatest operational impact.

- Officials noted that the full effects of fiscal year 2013 sequestration reductions on depot maintenance will likely not be known until sometime after the end of the fiscal year. However, in terms of statutory requirements, service officials believed they complied with the "50-50" provision in fiscal year 2013, and only the Army expected a shortfall in meeting core capability requirements.[19]

- The Office of the Secretary of Defense and service officials are particularly concerned that fiscal year 2013 depot maintenance impacts will be compounded if sequestration continues into future years or if reduced appropriations are enacted. Specifically, service officials are concerned about future (1) problems with equipment readiness shortfalls and delays in resetting the force, (2) increases in depot rates—leading to more expensive maintenance costs, and (3) impacts on depot workforce capabilities.

---

[19]According to Army officials, the expected shortfall in meeting core capability requirements was not solely due to sequestration, but also due to the high level of equipment readiness from previous maintenance efforts that reduced the need for additional depot maintenance.

Observations

Case Study 4: Base Operating Support

Background

Specific funding categories for base support vary by service but generally include

- Facilities Sustainment, Restoration, and Modernization (FSRM)
- Operating Support (activities to support operations and training, facilities management, warrior and family support programs, public safety and security services, environmental programs, information technology, logistics support, and other programs)

Planning Process

- Service installation commands and other organizations responsible for oversight of base operating support issued implementation guidance modeled on DOD and service-wide sequestration guidance. This guidance generally outlined areas where cuts could be implemented—such as building sustainment, delaying the renewal of contracts, and electricity usage and temperature controls—while protecting life, health, and safety.
- According to service officials, individual installation commanders retained substantial flexibility in how to implement cuts, including deciding which base support services to reduce or eliminate.

Actions Taken

Documentation from the services and interviews with officials show that many of the sequestration-related reductions focused on the FSRM account. These reductions included projects involving repairs and renovations of existing facilities and demolition of excess facilities.[20]

---

[20]We have reported challenges to DOD's ability to sustain and reduce excess facilities since designating this area as high-risk in 1997. Although we found that DOD made significant progress in addressing issues regarding sustainment of facilities, it continues to face significant challenges in reducing excess facilities (see GAO-13-283).

Observations
Case Study 4: Base Operating Support (cont.)

- In addition, documentation from the services shows reductions in other installation support services.[21] For example:

  - The Army, among other actions, reduced training offered to soldiers and families as part of the Army's Strong Bonds readiness and resiliency program[22] and reduced operating hours for entry points at an installation.

  - Air Force installations took a variety of actions depending on their circumstances, such as cancelling mold remediation and other environmental projects, deferring repairs to installation alarm systems for securing buildings and property, reducing recreation and fitness programs, and reducing chaplain services.

  - The Navy reduced sustainment of buildings, deferred restoration and demolition projects, and postponed port dredging where possible.

- Furthermore, some Army and Air Force installations, pursuant to certain statutory authorities, reduced the amount of appropriated fund support provided to Morale Welfare and Recreation activities operated by nonappropriated fund instrumentalities (NAFIs), resulting in changes to NAFI operations or fee structures. For example, according to Army and Air Force officials, some recreational swimming pools operated by NAFIs had previously received appropriated fund support for lifeguards but, due to sequestration, the NAFIs now pay those lifeguards with non-appropriated funds from pool fees.

---

[21]The exception to this is the Marine Corps, whose officials stated they did not take cuts in non-FSRM programs because those programs are already funded at the lowest acceptable level.
[22]The Army's Strong Bonds program is designed to provide soldiers and their families with skills needed to effectively address relationship challenges with a focus on prevention rather than treatment. The program administrators requested $93 million to support program events in fiscal year 2013, but received $40.5 million through September 2013. Army documentation shows that, due to sequestration, 3,024 Strong Bonds events were canceled in 2013, resulting in approximately 45,000 soldiers and their family members not receiving training through Strong Bonds. According to the Army, the Strong Bonds program was approximately $32 million short in comparison to the historical three-year average of $72 million for fiscal years 2010-2012.

Observations

Case Study 4: Base Operating Support (cont.)

Potential Impacts

- Service officials stated that sequestration-related reductions vary across installations.

- Service officials expressed concerns about future adverse effects resulting from current cuts and service reductions, such as delays in maintenance and deferral of facility investments.

  - Forgoing these expenditures now will likely lead to higher future costs due to facility degradation, according to service officials.

  - We previously reported that deferring sustainment of facilities will likely result in continued facility deterioration and higher future costs (e.g., see GAO-08-502 and GAO-09-336).

- DOD and service officials stated they are not planning to develop new metrics or tools to measure or assess sequestration impacts and will rely on existing measures, such as standards for delivery of installation support.

  - In response to four congressional mandates[23] and one congressional request, GAO will continue to monitor the impact of sequestration on the provision of base operating support.

---

[23]H.R. Rep. No.113-102 to accompany H.R. 1960 a bill for the National Defense Authorization Act of Fiscal Year 2014 (Jun. 7, 2013), at 122-124, 320, 322, and 324-325).

Case Study 5: Procurement and RDT&E

Figure 3: Fiscal Year 2013 Sequestration of Weapon System Acquisition Funds (RDT&E and Procurement) by Military Service[a]

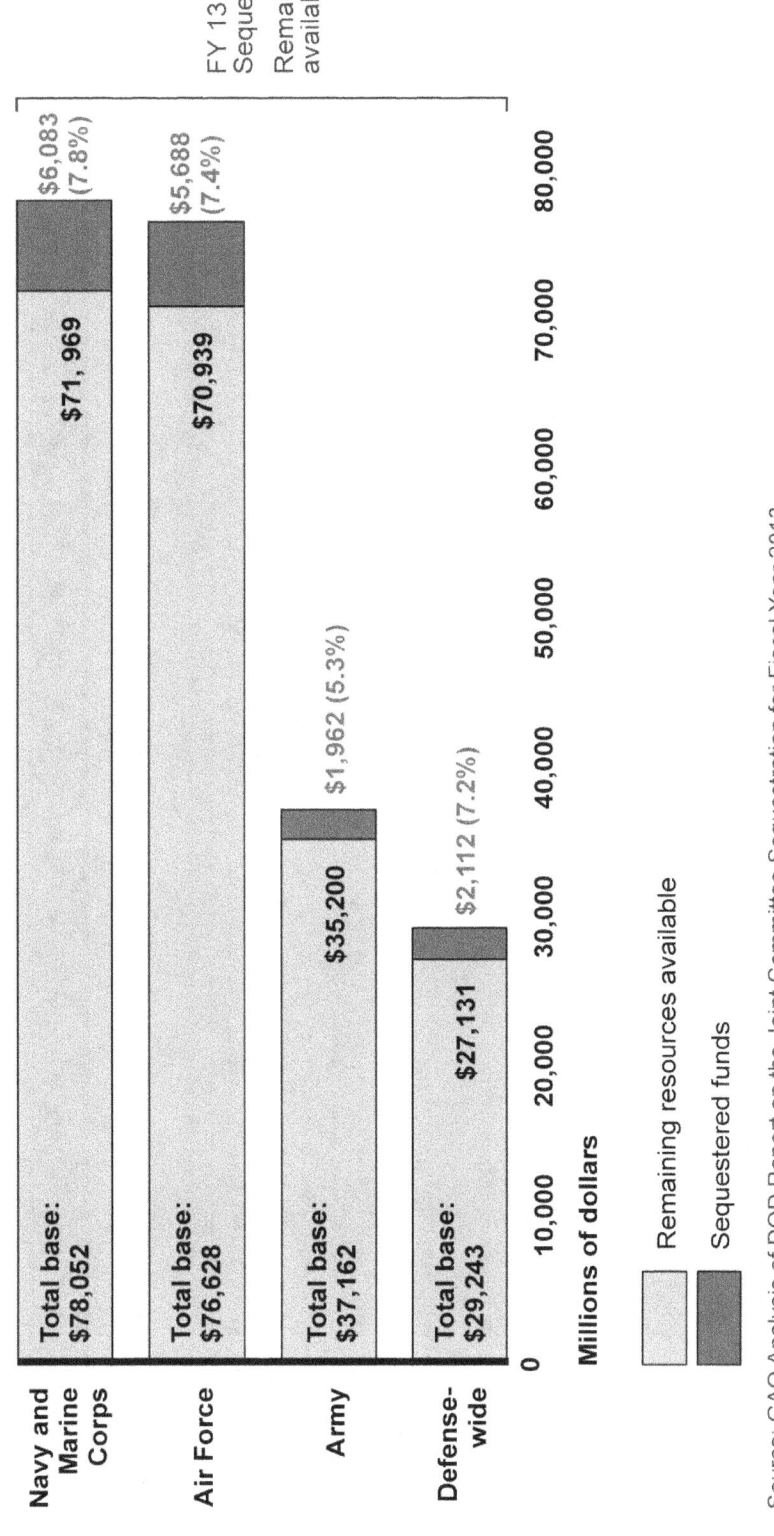

Navy and Marine Corps — Total base: $78,052 — $71,969 — $6,083 (7.8%)

Air Force — Total base: $76,628 — $70,939 — $5,688 (7.4%)

Army — Total base: $37,162 — $35,200 — $1,962 (5.3%)

Defense-wide — Total base: $29,243 — $27,131 — $2,112 (7.2%)

Millions of dollars (0, 10,000, 20,000, 30,000, 40,000, 50,000, 60,000, 70,000, 80,000)

FY 13 sequester base[b]: 221,084
Sequestered funds: – 15,845
Remaining resources available: $205,239

☐ Remaining resources available
■ Sequestered funds

Source: GAO Analysis of DOD Report on the Joint Committee Sequestration for Fiscal Year 2013.

[a] Totals may not add due to rounding.

[b] Base includes FY13 appropriation and prior year unobligated balances

Note: On March 1, 2013 OMB calculated the sequestrable base and reduction amounts based on the annualized amount set out in the continuing resolution then in effect. On March 26, 2013 the Consolidated and Further Continuing Appropriations Act, 2013 (Pub. L. No. 113-6) was enacted, providing different amounts of budget authority than were provided by the continuing resolution. According to DOD and OMB officials, the varying percentage reductions across the discretionary accounts are the result of differences between the annualized continuing resolution amounts used in OMB's March 1st report and the enacted full-year appropriations.

Table 2: Thirty Percent of Sequestered Funding Taken from Prior Year Unobligated Funds[a]

	Prior Years	Fiscal Year 2013
Procurement of Vehicles	64.6%	35.4%
Procurement of Aircraft	50.8%	49.2%
Procurement of Shipbuilding	50.5%	49.5%
Procurement of Ammunition	37.5%	62.5%
Procurement of Missiles	25.5%	74.5%
Other Procurement	17.0%	83.0%
Total Procurement	**42.1%**	**57.9%**
RDT&E	**10.5%**	**89.5%**
All Accounts	**30.0% ($4.8B)**	**70.0% ($11.1B)**

Source: GAO Analysis of DOD Report on the Joint Committee Sequestration for Fiscal Year 2013.

[a] Dollars rounded.

Observations

Case Study 5: Procurement and RDT&E (cont.)

Figure 4: DOD Views of the Fiscal Year 2013 Impacts of Sequestration on Selected RDT&E and Procurement Programs

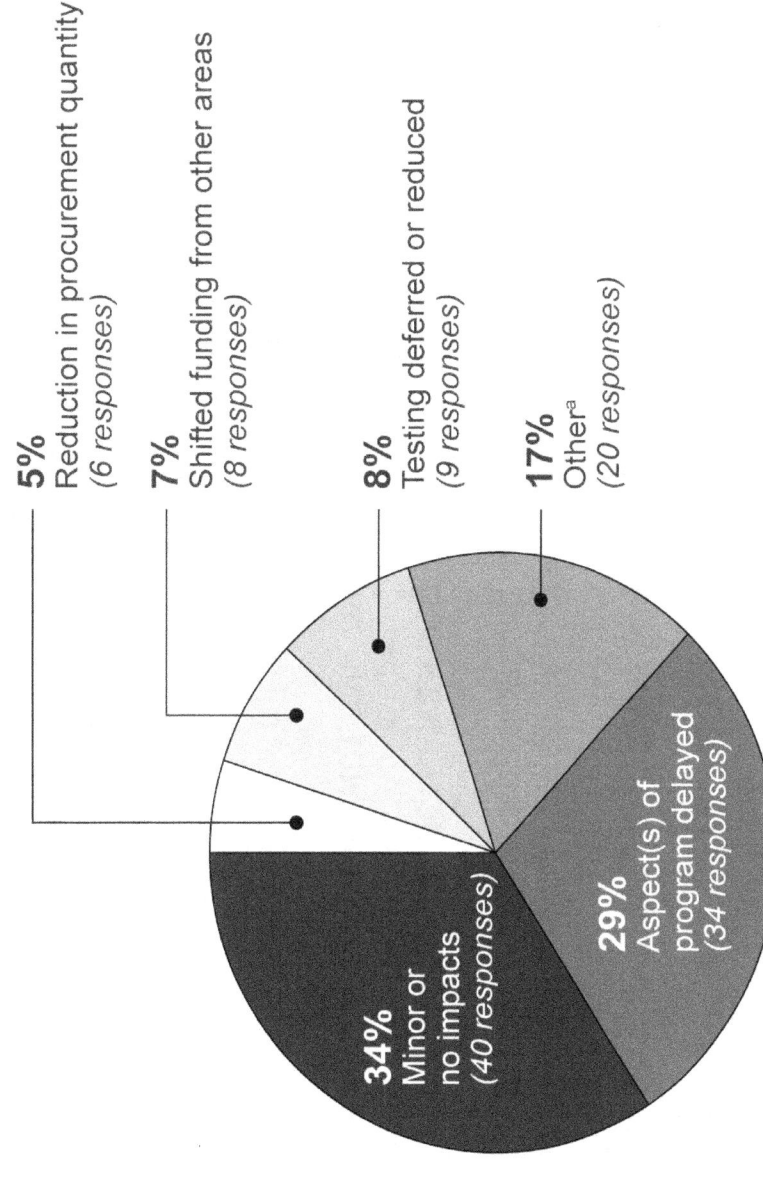

5%
Reduction in procurement quantity
(6 responses)

7%
Shifted funding from other areas
(8 responses)

8%
Testing deferred or reduced
(9 responses)

17%
Other[a]
(20 responses)

34%
Minor or no impacts
(40 responses)

29%
Aspect(s) of program delayed
(34 responses)

Source: GAO analysis of reported sequestration impacts on DOD RDT&E and procurement programs.

[a] Includes various program unique responses that did not fit into any other category, such as cancelation of a study or reductions of contractor support to programs.
Note: GAO asked 131 programs and 87 programs provided responses (May – Sept. 2013), identifying 117 total sequestration impacts. Some programs' responses fit into more than one category.

Observations

Case Study 5: Procurement and RDT&E (cont.)

Observations on Sequestration of Defense Investment Accounts

- Program decisions to offset sequestration generally did not appear to be arbitrary or overly severe and were typically short term.

  - No weapon system programs were cancelled and many programs reported minor or no impacts.

  - No programs reported cancelling or extensively changing program contracts.

  - Some programs reduced funding for activities that allowed for risk mitigation.

  - DOD officials agreed with this assessment.

- Budget lines/programs reduced or delayed efforts.

  - RDT&E budget lines/programs generally planned to reduce or delay research projects or system development and testing.

  - Procurement budget lines/programs typically planned to reduce weapon system quantities or defer modifications.

- DOD officials agreed that some decisions on offsetting sequestration reductions will result in bills that will need to be paid over the next few years, and for these and other reasons, sequestration reductions in fiscal year 2014, should they continue, may have more profound effects.

Observations

Case Study 5: Procurement and RDT&E (cont.)

Examples of Impacts on Specific Programs

- **Minor or no impact:** LHA (R) cut $70 million with no impact, because it was already funded over the contract price. KC-46 funded its $143 million reduction through funding set aside for possible engineering change orders.

- **Cuts that created delays:** F-35 Joint Strike Fighter will fund a portion of its reduction by delaying RDT&E work on software. The Evolved Expendable Launch Vehicle's reductions will result in deferred propulsion studies and travel and could reduce the ability to respond to unanticipated technical and support problems. Reductions to science and technology (defense-wide) funding resulted in a $64 million cut from multiple projects at universities and Federally Funded Research and Development Centers.

- **Cuts in quantity:** Apache Block III and Kiowa Warrior reductions will result in the loss of one aircraft each. The reductions to the DDG 51 Destroyer program may make it challenging to afford a 10th ship.

- **Cuts that will have to be paid back in the near future:** F-22 funding reductions will delay the start of a planned retrofit by 1 year. To prevent a break in production, the SSN 774 Virginia Class Submarine is funding its sequester reduction by using money originally planned for Government Furnished Equipment and testing activities. This money will eventually have to be replaced, since this equipment/work is still needed.

- GAO has an ongoing engagement that more broadly covers the impact(s) on RDT&E and procurement budget lines/programs as a result of sequestration reductions.

Observations: Objective 2

Use of Reprogramming and Transfer Authorities to Address Sequestration

- Subject to law and DOD financial management regulation, DOD has the authority to transfer funds between appropriation accounts and to reprogram funds within an appropriation account.

- The fiscal year 2013 full-year appropriations act provided DOD with $7.5 billion in broad transfer authority—$3.5 billion in special transfer authority for overseas contingency operations-related purposes and $4 billion in general transfer authority—that could be used, among other things, to address the impact of sequestration. This amount is generally consistent with the amounts of broad transfer authority provided to DOD in fiscal years 2011 and 2012.

- DOD guidance requires that the department seek prior approval from the congressional defense committees to reprogram funds above certain thresholds. For example, for funds appropriated in an O&M account, DOD guidance requires the department to seek prior approval if there is a cumulative increase or decrease greater than $15 million in a given budget activity. DOD submitted two requests to Congress dated May 17, 2013, totaling $9.4 billion, to transfer and reprogram fiscal year 2013 appropriated funds. According to DOD officials, these requests were primarily intended to offset potential shortfalls in fiscal year 2013 overseas contingency operations funding.

  - These requests proposed to transfer about $7.3 billion between accounts, using DOD's broad transfer authorities.

  - According to DOD officials, the remaining $2.1 billion represented large reprogrammings within budget accounts—which DOD guidance requires be submitted to the congressional committees for prior approval—and transfers from DOD's foreign currency fluctuations account.

Observations: Objective 2

Use of Reprogramming and Transfer Authorities to Address Sequestration (cont.)

- On July 19, 2013, DOD submitted two additional requests to Congress totaling about $1.5 billion. These requests identified replacement sources for the transfer or reprogramming requests previously disapproved by the congressional committees, as well as new requests to transfer and reprogram fiscal year 2013 funds.

- As of September 2013, DOD told us the relevant congressional committees had indicated agreement for $8.6 billion of DOD's total transfer and reprogramming requests and disapproved or deferred other aspects of DOD's requests, subject to continued review by those committees.

- DOD officials told us that, in addition to these "prior approval" requests, they expect the services to reprogram approximately $1-2 billion in fiscal year 2013 funds with existing authorities to address shifting priorities during budget execution.[24]

- According to DOD officials, these decisions were made by the services at the component level and are not included in the transfers and reprogrammings outlined above.

---

[24]Where the cumulative increase or decrease is within the thresholds established in DOD guidance, that guidance allows components to reprogram funds without prior approval. These reprogramming actions are referred to as "below threshold reprogramming actions".

Appendix I

Background on Statutes Related to Sequestration

- The **Balanced Budget and Emergency Deficit Control Act of 1985** (BBEDCA), Pub. L. No. 99-177 (1985) first authorized sequestration as a budget enforcement mechanism. Sequestration spending reductions are applied evenly across all programs, projects, and activities (PPAs) within a budget account.

- The **Budget Control Act of 2011** (BCA), Pub. L. No. 112-25 (2011) established, among other things:

  - A congressional Joint Select Committee on Deficit Reduction to propose legislation that would reduce federal deficits by $1.5 trillion over ten years (fiscal years 2012–2021).

  - A sequestration procedure originally to be ordered by the President on January 1, 2013 to ensure that the level of deficit reduction would be achieved in the event that the Joint Committee failed to reach agreement to reduce the deficit by at least $1.2 trillion, and an additional sequestration procedure triggered if appropriations exceed established discretionary spending caps in a given fiscal year between fiscal years 2012 and 2021. These spending reductions are applied uniformly between nonexempt defense and non-defense PPAs.

  - Certain defense-related programs, projects, and activities were exempt from sequestration, such as military personnel accounts[25] and the Department of Defense Medicare-Eligible Retiree Health Care Fund, as well as all programs administered by the Department of Veterans Affairs.

---

[25]BBEDCA permits the President (subject to certain requirements) to exempt military personnel accounts, and OMB notified Congress of the President's intent to do so in fiscal year 2013 on July 31, 2012.

Background on Statutes Related to Sequestration (cont.)

- The **Sequestration Transparency Act of 2012**, Pub. L. No. 112-155 (2012) directed the President to issue a report on sequestration; this report was to include identifying all exempt and nonexempt accounts. As a result, on September 14, 2012, OMB issued a report that identified the sequestration percentage reduction as 9.4 percent for nonexempt defense discretionary funding and 10.0 percent for nonexempt defense direct spending programs.[26]

  - Nonexempt defense discretionary programs include the services' operation and maintenance (O&M) appropriations. Examples of nonexempt defense direct spending accounts are certain accounts related to the administrative and infrastructure costs of commissary operations.

- The **American Taxpayer Relief Act of 2012**, Pub. L. No. 112-240 (2013) delayed the Joint Committee sequestration until March 1, 2013 and amended the discretionary spending caps for fiscal year 2013. As a result, OMB recalculated the reduction as 7.8 percent for nonexempt defense discretionary funding and 7.9 percent for nonexempt defense direct spending programs.

  - On March 1, 2013, the President ordered sequestration, as required by law, because the Joint Select Committee on Deficit Reduction had not reached agreement.

---

[26]Discretionary programs are typically funded annually through the congressional appropriations process. Mandatory programs, also known as "pay-as-you-go" or PAYGO programs are direct spending or entitlement programs. This is budget authority typically authorized by permanent law, rather than annual appropriations acts. The Military Retirement and Medicare-Eligible Retiree Health Care Funds are examples of DOD-specific direct spending programs (although these two programs are exempt from sequestration).

Enclosure II: GAO Contacts and Staff Acknowledgments

GAO Contacts

Sharon L. Pickup, (202) 512-9619 or pickups@gao.gov; Michael J. Sullivan, (202) 512-4841 or sullivanm@gao.gov

Staff Acknowledgments

In addition to the contacts named above, Brenda Farrell, Director; Brian Lepore, Director; Zina Merritt, Director; Lori Atkinson, Assistant Director; Bruce Fairbairn, Assistant Director; Tom Gosling, Assistant Director; J. Kristopher Keener, Assistant Director; Mark Pross, Assistant Director; Bruce Thomas, Assistant Director; Matthew Ullengren, Assistant Director; Jennifer Andreone; Natalya Barden; Russell Bryan; R. Eli DeVan; Chaneé Gaskin; Laura Hook; LaToya King; Joanne Landesman; Brian Mazanec; Meghan Perez; Janine Prybyla; Jeanett Reid; Amber Lopez Roberts; Traye Smith; Don Springman; Maria Storts; Walter Vance; and Michael Willems made significant contributions to this report.

(351822)

GAO's Mission	The Government Accountability Office, the audit, evaluation, and investigative arm of Congress, exists to support Congress in meeting its constitutional responsibilities and to help improve the performance and accountability of the federal government for the American people. GAO examines the use of public funds; evaluates federal programs and policies; and provides analyses, recommendations, and other assistance to help Congress make informed oversight, policy, and funding decisions. GAO's commitment to good government is reflected in its core values of accountability, integrity, and reliability.
Obtaining Copies of GAO Reports and Testimony	The fastest and easiest way to obtain copies of GAO documents at no cost is through GAO's website (www.gao.gov). Each weekday afternoon, GAO posts on its website newly released reports, testimony, and correspondence. To have GAO e-mail you a list of newly posted products, go to www.gao.gov and select "E-mail Updates."
Order by Phone	The price of each GAO publication reflects GAO's actual cost of production and distribution and depends on the number of pages in the publication and whether the publication is printed in color or black and white. Pricing and ordering information is posted on GAO's website, http://www.gao.gov/ordering.htm. Place orders by calling (202) 512-6000, toll free (866) 801-7077, or TDD (202) 512-2537. Orders may be paid for using American Express, Discover Card, MasterCard, Visa, check, or money order. Call for additional information.
Connect with GAO	Connect with GAO on Facebook, Flickr, Twitter, and YouTube. Subscribe to our RSS Feeds or E-mail Updates. Listen to our Podcasts. Visit GAO on the web at www.gao.gov.
To Report Fraud, Waste, and Abuse in Federal Programs	Contact: Website: www.gao.gov/fraudnet/fraudnet.htm E-mail: fraudnet@gao.gov Automated answering system: (800) 424-5454 or (202) 512-7470
Congressional Relations	Katherine Siggerud, Managing Director, siggerudk@gao.gov, (202) 512-4400, U.S. Government Accountability Office, 441 G Street NW, Room 7125, Washington, DC 20548
Public Affairs	Chuck Young, Managing Director, youngc1@gao.gov, (202) 512-4800 U.S. Government Accountability Office, 441 G Street NW, Room 7149 Washington, DC 20548

www.ingramcontent.com/pod-product-compliance
Lightning Source LLC
Chambersburg PA
CBHW081707310526
45790CB00021B/2901